HOW TO THRIVE IN A BAD ECONOMY

LUCY RUTH

I dedicate this book to God who gave me wisdom to write and empower others. To my mom in heaven, I never had the chance to say goodbye and I will always love you. To my family, friends and networks. I love you all.

CONTENTS

ISBN-978-19990814-6-1

Publisher's Note

INTRODUCTION

Welcome to 2020. The year was celebrated by many on January 1st, and little did anyone know that the year would turn into one of the worst years millennials have ever experienced. At the beginning of the year, we all made resolutions on how we would succeed and accompany our goals. Well, the universe had other plans. We experienced an earthquake in the name of a virus called Corona, also known as Covid19. The virus that took the lives of thousands of people and made businesses and everyone to lose. We all lost one way or the other.

The world has experienced natural disasters, but never has the whole world been shaken like this. So in times like these where we have been stripped and laid bare by a virus. We must rebuild and renovate our old lives. Do you remember the wildfire disasters where wildfire burns and destroys an entire forest? If you revisit the same forest after a couple of years, that forest will bloom again with fresh vegetation, and it replenishes itself also organically.

To remind you as earthquakes happen, so do health pandemics. Look at the article below, which I found on Wikipedia about the Spanish flu, which occurred over 100 years ago. One thing I can say is our generation is blessed to have fast ways of spreading communications, which makes it easy to convey messages in times of emergencies.

CHAPTER ONE

The Spanish Flu

The Spanish flu (also known as the 1918 flu pandemic) was an unusually deadly influenza pandemic. Lasting from January 1918 to December 1920, it infected 500 million people—about a quarter of the world's population at the time. The death toll is estimated to have been anywhere from 17 million to 50 million, and possibly as high as 100 million, making it one of the deadliest pandemics in human history.

To maintain morale, World War I censors minimized early reports of illness and mortality in Germany, the United Kingdom, France, and the United States. Newspapers were free to report the epidemic's effects in neutral Spain, such as the grave illness of King Alfonso XIII, and these stories created a false impression of Spain as especially hard hit.] This gave rise to the name Spanish flu Historical and epidemiological data are inadequate to identify with certainty the pandemic's geographic origin, with varying views as to its location.

Most influenza outbreaks disproportionately kill the very young and the very old, with a higher survival rate for those in between those age groups. Still, the Spanish flu pandemic resulted in a higher than expected mortality rate for young adults. Scientists offer several possible explanations for the high mortality rate of the 1918 influenza pandemic. Some analyses have shown the virus to be particularly deadly because it triggers a cytokine storm, which ravages the more reliable immune system of young adults. In contrast, a 2007 analysis of medical journals from the period of the pandemic found that the viral infection was no more aggressive than previous influenza strains. Instead, malnourishment, overcrowded medical camps and hospitals, and poor hygiene promoted bacterial superinfection. This superinfection killed most of the victims, typically after a somewhat prolonged death bed. (Source Wikipedia)

Survival Tips

Here are some survival tips to get you going until you rebound again. The reason why I shared the article above is to keep you motivated. These things happen, and sometimes, in my opinion, is nature's way of resetting itself. We will rebound and be prosperous.

The first thing to start doing immediately is to learn how to survive with what you have. I learned a few days ago that I was spending too much during the isolation because my kids kept eating way too many snacks that provided zero nutritional value and would run out fast.

Ditch buying snacks, and make your home-cooked snacks, bake some bread, cookies, or your children's favorite baked meal from home.

Divorce your coffee runs and make your coffee in the comfort of your home. Stop paying for a gym membership and expensive phone contracts. You don't need a new phone; you can have an old phone for up to three years. I don't have cable as Netflix and YouTube are enough. Every little will help you save money.

There are zero reasons why one should be hungry after eating something that fills one up, fills them, and makes them full; I also encourage homemade popcorn for snacks. I found potato soup, butternut soup, and even mixed bean soup to be very filling. My kids used to hate bean soup until my daughter suffered constipation. She was in pain and during that moment I said to her it's because you don't eat beans. She now loves beans. Beans are high in fiber and keep them full for long. If you don't know how to make bean soup, Pinterest has lots of ideas. Drop me an email at info@lucyruth.page for a bean soup recipe.

Once your child transitions from eating cookies, chips, and other unhealthy snacks to soup, then they will adjust and be fuller for longer. Encourage your children to drink more water. Water is filling and healthy. It eliminates a buy item from your shopping list.

Bean Soup

Fall in love with your favorite bean type and make a habit of making bean soup for your children. Some beans produce a lot of gas. If you have gas problems, use beano. It's a gas pill that helps reduce gas. Take it before you eat gassy foods. Beans are rich in fiber, iron, copper, and magnesium. They are rich in nutrients.

Homemade Banana Pancakes

Invest in made at home foods. See the picture below. When you make your food, you save money with food prices skyrocketing. The one thing you must do is make your food. Did you know that fast food costs more money than made at home? The Corona Virus has caused havoc, and with airlines going out of business, it's undoubtedly going to make food expensive. Have a food budget. The pancakes below require two cups of flour, three ripe bananas, a lit bit of sugar, and you are good to go. By making simple life changes, you save money and also protect your health. Head over to Pinterest and happy banana recipe pinning!

Create Your Own Salads

I mixed cucumber, carrot, tomatoes, lettuce, and chopped in some mangoes to make this salad. This is one of my favorite salads to make. It's not a bland salad. The flavors create a taste that can be enjoyed without the use of dressing. Feel free to make your salad dressing from scratch.

Introduce Avocados To Your Children

Not only do avocados make excellent guacamole, but avocados can also go on crackers, toast, or merely an avocado salad. This food fills you and makes you full for long, thereby reducing the amount of snacking, and that saves money in the long run. Stop buying junk.

Stop Unnecessary Spending

Whilst clicking to get what you want online is ideal, watch your spending. Stop using your credit cards immediately unless it's an emergency. You save money by not paying interest. Stop frequenting the stores for groceries. Buy enough food to last you until your next payday. The more we go to the store, the more we spend. By cutting the number of grocery store visits, we save money. Buy what you need and shop with a list.

Fall In Love With Less Is More

On March 24th, I moved after selling my house. Whilst packing, I couldn't believe that I had so many clothes, and so did my kids. We need to learn to repurpose our clothes and buy out of need instead of out of desire, especially if you have to use your credit cards. The fewer clothes you have, the more money saved.

Renovate your Finances

Whilst dealing with the trauma of losing your job, DO NOT fall prey to bogus work from home opportunities where you have to spend lots of money before you make money. Do your research before giving away your credit card details. Whilst technology has made life more accessible for people to connect, it has unfortunately also made it easier for scammers and criminals to take care of the variables. You don't need to leave the house to lose money as technology has made it easy to access information and connect with everyone literally.

I learned the hard way. I used to sign up for free trial apps, and then forget to cancel them on time. I once forgot to cancel a free trial app that I never used, and it cost me $75. Cancel unnecessary subscriptions.

If you have lost your job and are struggling to make ends meet, talk to a financial advisor or a credit counseling agency. There are ways to get things in order by doing debt consolidation. Having too much debt can trigger depression. Stop worrying about credit scores and concentrate on the basics that you need to get by. Make payment arrangements. Talk to your creditors about your situation.

With time life gets better. Before you buy something new, check marketplaces in your area. In Canada, we have Kijiji. It's a platform where one can find free stuff before spending money on a new item. Buy second hand, and if your food budget is low find food banks in your area. Invest in free activities during the summer months and in the winter. This allows you to spend money on the necessities that one needs whilst in dire financial situations. Sell secondhand items in your house. Renovate all the areas of your life.

Debunking Debt!

To avoid debt, first, you must get rid of debt cards sugarcoated as credit cards. Debit cards are named debit because you are debiting from your wallet. If they advertised credit cards as debt cards, maybe our thinking will be different.

Stop borrowing and stop worrying about credit scores. During the financial crisis, do not fall prey to shark loans, which offer ridiculous interest rates. This will only make your debt bigger. If you are struggling to pay your bills, talk to a financial advisor. You cannot borrow yourself out of debt. Incorporate the snowball method to reduce the amount of debt.

What Is The Snowball Method?

The Snowball method is a formula used to eliminate debt by paying accounts with the smallest debt first. One is advised to pay off small balances first. You will need to pay the minimum payment for the more significant debts as well. Once the small balances are paid off, then you have eliminated a bill and can now pay the more significant balances with the extra money you currently have.

CHAPTER TWO

Ways to Generate Additional Income

Start Your Own Childcare Business

Childcare business is a demanding business. You must have the willpower to do it. With proper planning and research, one can start a thriving childcare center and make money whilst providing care for society's most valuable assets. Despite different backgrounds, childcare is universal. To start, you will need to plan your menus and buy food supplies, possibly from Costco or your local food wholesaler. You will also need toys, plan your day, and create a schedule. Planning, a goodnight's sleep, and lots of patience are all you need.

When babysitting toddlers, you need to keep them busy with activity. I used to run a daycare in my home. How I did it was, I would take them to community centers in different schools where they offered playtime for stay at home mothers and their tots. They usually allow childcare givers to come to connect, learn, and play for the kids. Check with your local city or library for fun activities for toddlers. Also, check your municipality's community activity guide. These activities are free.

A simple way of childminding is providing before and after school childcare or summer babysitting when schools are out. It's all about your willingness and dedication to it. Use the internet for resources. Ask Uncle G (Google). He knows it all. This allows you to spend money on the necessities that one needs whilst in a bad financial situation.

The good news about the 20th century is that you don't need to leave your house to make money. I have heard speakers say real wealth will start when you start working for yourself. With the rise of digital marketing, one can begin to sell and promote anything in the comfort of their own home. Imagine choosing when and how you want to work? Now is the time to start using your skills and experience in working for yourself. If you work in an office and are good at administrative tasks, you can create your account on Freelancer, Fiverr, and many more as a virtual assistant, accountant, or even offer online tutoring on the subjects you know best. Facebook and Instagram are profitable channels of growing your business and marketing yourself.

Start A Dropshipping Business

Drop shipping is the new norm for new entrepreneurs in the digital era.

The advantage of drop shipping is that one does not need to pre-order bulk stock. You get paid when someone buys your products. Companies like Shopify, Amazon, and Printify are great places to get you started.

Focus On Your Dream

You will need to stay focused to achieve your hustle. Try and remember that not every business has to grow big. There will be hiccups along the way. If at first, you don't succeed, try, try, and try again using different methods. I also recommend checking affiliate marketing to make money. Affiliate marketing is trending in the digital era. Find a niche, market, and bang! You have residual income.

Practice P's of the Pursuit of Prosperity

Passion - Have a burning desire to pursue your idea. When the plan is passion-driven, it makes it easy to reach organic growth. When you are passionate about an idea, you are not ashamed to share and be heard. Every time I write a book, I get excited to share my work. Passion builds resilience, and with resilience, you can come out of any setbacks. Passion is powerful because it is original and cannot be replicated. Stay the course, and make sure the passion turns to profit.

Persistence - an example of persistence is how you log

onto your social media accounts. Use that formula to post and promote your hustle on social media consistently. The future is digital, so invest in growing a following and grow organically. Find and attract persistent business networking groups and collaborate. Persistence is the golden key to success. When you apply this type of persistency, you automatically use the P of Promotion whilst being persistent

Patience- is a virtue, said the wise men. Patience will take you far not only in bustling but in life. As a writer, the first book I wrote, I did not make money. I started making money on my second book and third book. Had I lost patience because of my first experience; I would not be writing this book. I write because I have a passion for writing, I am persistent in the journey, and I remain focused. I continuously remind myself that J.K. Rowling lived a rag to riches life on which she worked hard to get to billionaire status. She earned it, and so can you and I.

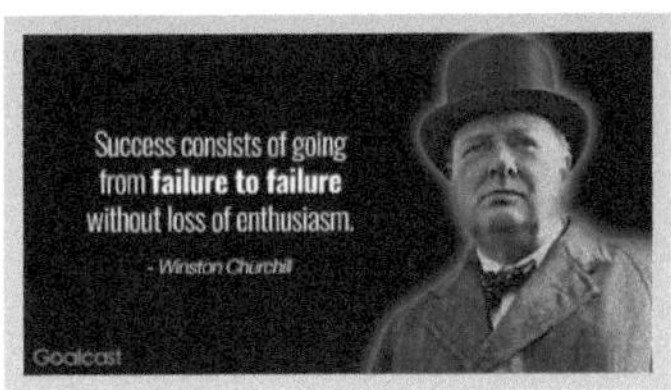

Learn A New Skill

We now live in a world where working using your hands is the way to success. With the rise of construction and technology, there is a shortage of skilled people all over the world. Being skilled gives you an advantage over a lot of people because you are one of a kind. If you have a passion for painting or carpentry, join the skilled trades industry, and get paid big bucks whilst doing your hobby.

I happen to be one of the few women in the skilled trades industry. I went to college in 2017 and studied CNC Programming. I am experienced enough that I don't fear losing my job, and 99% of the time, the jobs look for me. Almost every industry uses different versions of CNC machines for making parts and equipment. According to Zip Recruiter, "As of May 4, 2020, the average annual pay for a CNC Programmer in the United States is $57,252 a year. While ZipRecruiter sees annual salaries as high as $86,000 and as low as $31,000, the majority of CNC Programmer salaries currently range between $46,500 (25th percentile) to $64,500 (75th percentile) across the United States." With experience, the CNC industry pays a lot of money. (glassdoor.com) I am blessed enough to have won the job lottery. I have the experience, and the opportunities are endless.

I am also skilled in terms of design using Solidworks. If you have a love for designing, consider IT and mechanical design.

Bake N' Sell

Some people are skilled at baking and can monetize this gift. You can have a side hustle baking quality or even organic goods to a niche market. The good thing about baked goods or any cooking is once you have a customer base, they keep returning as the need for perishables recycles with each day, week, and month. I bake different goods and sell them at Christmas markets to make extra income. The more you use your talents, the more you will always have something that brings you profit. The ideas are endless. All you need is time and dedication. Social media marketplaces have made it easy for our generation to sell items, so use it wisely.

You Can Also...

- Make money by renting a spare bedroom in your house for a student if you have finished the basement and its lying idle. Rent it out. The advantage of renting a room to students is that

the rooms are occupied for a short term, and
when your financial situation improves, then
you can always not renew the short-term lease.

- Sell secondhand items in your house. Renovate
all the areas of your life.
- Use your skill and experience to start an online
business working for yourself.
- Use staffing agencies to find a side job to sustain
you whilst starting. Staffing agencies usually
work around your availability. You choose the
days when you want to work.
- Consider starting a cleaning company that is
competitive.Companies more than ever are
going to need professional cleaners. Healthcare
industry cleaning standards are higher than
before so they need more people.
- Register with Uber and work when it suits you
to create additional income. All you need is
your car and insurance.

CHAPTER THREE

Become a Foster Parent or Provide Respite Care

Foster parents provide a stable and caring home that encourages a child's growth and development. In Ontario, foster families can care for up to four children at a time. Foster parents are people who have a genuine desire to contribute to a child and youth's well-being, and their community, and come from all cultural and religious backgrounds. (canada.ca) Check with your city's municipalities for your location.

By providing respite care, you are providing relief to caregivers who take care of the elders or those who suffer from disabilities. This can be done in your own home. Contact your local authorities or children's services about how you can start should you wish to provide care. I inquired with my local agency, and one of the requirements they needed was that the person has their own room, and also there must be a fire alarm on each level of your dwelling. The pay for this is pretty rewarding. One is required to have patience and must have a caring heart.

Create Habits Of Happiness

Imagine going through a hard time and feeling unhappy with your life? Whether losing your job or whatever circumstance you are in, being depressed is hard enough. It would help if you created habits of happiness to go through this new norm.

When we focus our minds with positive thoughts, we will achieve great things. To acquire habits of joy, you must first let go of yesterday and embrace today.

Let go of things and situations that you cannot change and stop worrying. By accepting the position you are in now, you avoid unnecessary stress; we all know that stress is terrible, so why feed it? I have a poem in my house which my aunt gifted me when she visited me in Canada from England, and it reads, "God grant me the serenity to accept the things I cannot change, the courage to change the things I can and wisdom to know the difference."

Below are a few examples one can do daily to create your happiness.

- Create a daily to-do list.
- Create a habit of exercising daily, start with twenty minutes, and improve at a steady pace.
- Practice meditation. Take time away from gadgets and electronics and breathe in and out. YouTube is the place to go for videos. Start doing it by watching the video until you can do it by yourself.
- Watch comedy and laugh every day. I read a quote saying that six-year old's laugh 300 times a day and adults only laugh 16-100 times a day. So it's essential to add laughter to our daily schedules. Laughter releases good endorphins in our bodies.
- Get adequate sleep all the time, go to bed at the same time, and wake up at the same time; this will help you achieve your daily habits. We all know that when we sleep-deprived, we get grumpy and even headaches.
- Get some fresh air by opening windows or by simply walking outside.

- Volunteer with your favorite charity a couple of times a year.
- Have faith every day and live a life of expectancy and gratitude. Expect miracles and be grateful for everything you have. I always say a prayer to God thanking him for the blessings that are here today, and the blessings that are to come. I am thankful for food every day.
- Write and document your good thoughts, who knows you might be the next great motivational speaker.
- Read books that align with who you are and your beliefs.
- Have a hobby and be yourself. Embrace the new norm and tell yourself that life gets better.

Mental Health Wellness In The Storms Of Life

Not only have people lost jobs, but people have also lost loved ones due to COVID-19. All of a sudden, you find yourself hopeless, and you can't function. Your brain cannot take it. You are overwhelmed. I am here to give you hope that this season shall pass. Although lives cannot be replaced, life gets better. Join social platforms that provide you with hope. Reach out and talk to your family and friends and let them know how you feel. Talk to your doctor or health clinics. The dark cloud that you were facing will turn grey before it turns white, and eventually, you will have a clear sky, clear sky in your mental state. I encourage you to find a church and reach out. During our darkest moments, one finds themselves not wanting to talk; we question the existence of God, we think that God doesn't love us. I can testify that I have walked that journey, and no one can ever understand this journey except you. I lost my mother to suicide at the age of ten, and I was hopeless for so many years. I hated events, and I repeatedly asked God why I had to go through this journey. I understand this journey very well, and I can tell you that with time, you will heal. You will heal at your own pace. I am available to listen and, on special occasions, a call—email in confidence to info@lucyruth.page.

How To Cope With The Financial Depression

In these trying times, try to avoid addictive activities, like gambling. They become habit-forming. Please see below a study that was done in Greece during the recession.

The economic crisis in Greece was found to have linked mental health-related issues. Many people suffered from depression, and some were suicidal.

See study below

In 2013, we conducted a nationwide telephone survey, following the same methodology of previous surveys (2–4), in order to identify the general population's strategies for tackling increasing financial demands. A random and representative sample of 2,188 people were interviewed about their financial difficulties, ways of dealing with financial strain, and the presence of major depression and suicidality. A major depression diagnosis was ascertained by the pertinent module of the Structured Clinical Interview (5), while financial burden was assessed through the Index of Personal Economic Distress (2).

Interestingly, 2% of the population reported that they resort to gambling in order to deal with financial distress. A series of univariate analyses were performed to identify the variables that bore a statistically significant association with gambling: they were gender, educational status, employment status, financial distress and working hours. A logistic regression analysis with the aforementioned variables entered as predictors and gambling as the outcome variable (binary: yes/no) indicated that financial distress and working hours were the only variables exerting an independent effect on gambling. In particular, for every unit increase in the Index of Personal Economic Distress, respondents were 1.12 times more likely to gamble in order to deal with financial strain (OR=1.12, 95% CI: 1.03-1.23). Furthermore, participants who reported working more than 40 hours per week were roughly 7 times more likely to gamble than those who reportedly work less (OR=7.34, 95% CI: 2.03-22.91).

A non-significantly lower prevalence of major depression was found among respondents who reported they gamble as a way of dealing with financial difficulties (0.9% among those who gamble vs. 16.3% among those who do not, df (1)=0.63, p>0.05). With regard to suicidality, 0% of people who reported that they gamble experienced suicidal ideation, in contrast to 2.6% among people who do not gamble: df (1)=1.15, p>0.05).

Although differences were not significant, these data

suggest that gambling offers an alternative to the dead-end created by the grim financial reality in Greece, buffering to some extent against hopelessness, a strong risk factor for major depression, suicidality and suicide (6–8). However, the existing literature suggests that, when gambling turns into its pathological form, it progresses through four stages: winning, losing, desperation and hopelessness (9). Thus, while it seems initially to offer a solution, it may subsequently lead to the same dead-end it wishes to avoid.

These data add to the growing literature (10,11) about the impact of recession on the mental health of the Greek population and the need for actions which are tailored to the specific characteristics of each population subgroup.

ARTICLE INFORMATION

World Psychiatry. 2014 Oct; 13(3): 324.
Published online 2014 Oct 1. doi: 10.1002/wps.20156
PMCID: PMC4219078
PMID: 25273310

There are many organizations to help you get through this fleeting season. Find a new hobby or study an online course to keep you occupied or busy. Move-in with close friends and relatives, not only do you save money but the social aspect of having family, company, and support as well.

Find charities or volunteer in older people's homes or schools. They usually require a police check. Create a club where you and your friends play organized sports like badminton, volleyball, tennis, pool, darts, and many more? This will give you something to look forward to.

Be content, and don't be greedy. Allow organic growth as organic is sustainable.

Try doing these fantastic ideas to reduce stress and anxiety.

Became artistic, everyone is an artist. Find your talent, be it playing the guitar, writing books, writing songs, painting, etc.

Create memories of your life, make a movie about your experience using apps like iMovie.

Develop new ideas by learning what's trending every month via google trends.

Embrace speed bumps and slow down when overwhelmed.

Feed your mind the right content.

Please get rid of clutter in your garage, basement, and closets and most of all declutter your devices lol (my sense of humor)

Heal, have hope that life gets better.

Here are a few quotes to motivate you through the journey of entrepreneurship. Yes You Can!

"You can't get there by bus, only hard work,risking, and by not quite knowing what you are doing. What you will discover will be wonderful: yourself."

Alan Alder

Buddhist saying...
"Always deliver more than expected."

Larry Page

"Find the tribe that matches your vibe."

Women's Network

"I will win, not immediately but definitely "

Leonardo Decaprio

" Your attitude will determine your Altitude."

Proverb

All the best and you can do it!

Unknown

ABOUT THE AUTHOR

Lucy is an author and a public speaker. She is a Guinness World Record Holder. Her first book titled "Debunk & Develop Your Mind" was published on March 28, 2019 and became a #1 bestseller on Amazon. Her second book was titled "How to Love Yourself after Bullying and Abuse" . She has also written her third book coming out April 15 2020 called "How to Live your Life in Reverse."

Her efforts to inspire those in her community and abroad have led to networking opportunities

with many public figures who have endorsed her work.

She is a mother of three, works fulltime and also runs an online business selling African heritage

products on Amazon. In 2018, Lucy was featured in a story by The Weight She Carries for her support of African artistry.

The trajectory of her life changed at the age of ten when she lost her mother in her native,

Zimbabwe. For years, Lucy struggled with depression and felt alone because depression was not a topic people discussed in Zimbabwe. This birthed a desire to connect with people.

Having lived and worked in three continents: Africa, Europe and now North America, Lucy has been exposed to different cultures and experiences. While customs vary, she has seen a common thread in every place she has lived; the challenges people face are the same.

Gifted in being a good listener, Lucy is the voice of those who cannot stand up for themselves.

She is passionate about equal opportunities for all and the empowerment of all people.

Lucy has an ongoing relationship with the prison and is working on creating a self-help course

for women who have served their time to rise and become tomorrow's leaders Lucy manages and moderates a growing group for Strong Women on Facebook which has 425, 000 women worldwide.

Lucy has a vision to empower and young men and women to believe in themselves and chase their dreams.

Lucy is also part of the Toronto Women's Expo 2020 organizing committee.

The expo and charity Gala in partnership with MIllion dollar smiles charity which builds

playgrounds for sick kids countrywide.

Some of her notable accomplishments include:

- KeynoteSpeakerfortheWellandBlackHistoryMonth2019
- Keynote Speaker for Mother's Day at K.I.M Toronto
- Speaker at Grand Valley Women's Prison
- Speaker at Women's Economic Forum London 2019
- Speaker at Edo Women Conference Jan 2020
- Guest on Nebo TV speaking on mental health
- Guest on Arise F.M. (Christian Radio)
- Award Nominee for Women making an impact Egypt March 2020

In addition, Lucy has experience in airport operations, education in airline and travel and is a holder of 30 IATA points. She also has education in events management with public relations.

Thanks for reading. If you enjoyed this book, please consider leaving an honest review on your favorite store."